Nanaboozhoo Babaamosed

Nanaboozhoo Went Walking and Other Stories from Grand Portage

Grand Portage Band of Lake Superior Chippewa
P.O. Box 428 Grand Portage, MN 55605
83 Stevens Rd Grand Portage

Book Design and Cover by Erin Leary

Nanaboozhoo Babaamosed: Nanaboozhoo Went Walking and Other Stories from Grand Portage

Second Edition 2024

ISBN: 978-1-7365519-7-4

Hidden Timber Books
6650 West State Street #D98
Milwaukee, WI 53213
www.hiddentimberbooks.com

Ordering information: Special discounts are available on quantity purchases by corporations, associations, and others. For details, contact the publisher at the address above.

Orignal cover for *Be-Inabin / Come Look* (1976)

Publication Information

First Editions

Stories originally published as part of the Bilingual Reading Series, Ojibwe Cultural Resource Center of Independent School District № 166.

Director and Editor: Billy Blackwell

Be-Inabin / Come Look (1976)

"Nanabozho and the Birch Trees" – Storyteller Billy Blackwell, Grand Portage

"Shi-me - The Lost Boy" – Storyteller Liza Thibault, Grand Portage

"The Boy Who Turned Into a Robin" – Ogimabinaysik, Mille Lacs

Artwork – Jim Korf, Moose Valley, Hovland Minnesota

Elementary Ed. Writing Specialist – Aune Fadum, Duluth, Minnesota

Nanabozho Babamoset / Nanabozho Went Walking (1977)

"Nanabozho and the Beavers"

"Nanabozho and the Ducks"

"Nanabozho and the Red Willows"

These three stories were all told by Dakos of Grand Portage.

Special acknowledgement to Amelia Legarde for the Ojibwe language translations.

Nanabozho

"Pakiwis" - Storyteller Alec Bushman, Bebamigeeshig, Grand Portage, with Ojibwe translation by Liza Thibault, Grand Portage

"The Theft of Fire" - Storyteller Billy Blackwell, Wabanakwad, Grand Portage with Ojibwe translation by Amelia Legarde

Second Edition

Nanaboozhoo Babaamosed: Nanaboozhoo Went Walking and Other Stories from Grand Portage

Double Vowel Transcription: Margaret Noodin & Michael Zimmerman, Jr.

Editor: Erik Martin Redix

These are traditional Ojibwe stories collected from the Anishinaabeg.

We ask that in keeping with our Ojibwe customs they are not read in the summertime or late spring or early fall.

Nanaboozhoo stories can only be told when there is snow on the ground and the thunders have gone to the south.

We tell all sacred stories in winter only and we tell all other stories any time we are learning.

The other stories, other than Nanaboozhoo stories, can be told anytime.

Contents

The Theft of Fire

Ningoding bibooning, Nanaboozhoo ogii-wiidabimaan ookomisan biinji-wiigiwaaming. "Ingii-noondaan dibaajimotaagwag ishkode," gii-ikido Nanaboozhoo. "Wegonen aawang? Booch ji-wanendaman," gii-nakwetaminid ookomisan. "Gaawiin, gaawiin, booch ji-gikendamaan," gii-nakwetawaad Nanaboozhoo, "Booch ji-gikendamaan."

One winter day, Nanaboozhoo sat inside the wigwam with his grandmother. "I have heard about fire," said Nanaboozhoo. "What is it?" "You must forget about it," answered his old grandmother. "No, no. I must know," replied Nanaboozhoo, "I must know."

"Giishpin sa memindage wii-kikendaman," ookomisan gii-nakwetaagod, "aawan gegoo ji-giizhizigooyang. Bezhig akiwenzi miinawaa niizh odaanisima' dash ganawendamowaad. Danakiiwag minising zaaga'iganing. Gichi-gashki'ewizi dash a'aw akiwenzi. Gaawiin dash obagidinaasiin awiiyan ji-gimoodinid ishkode."

"Well, if you must know," his grandmother replied, "it is something to keep us warm. It is guarded by an old man and his two daughters. They live on an island in the lake. But the old man is powerful. He will not let anyone steal the fire from him."

“Gaawiin ingashki-wanendanziin,” Nanaboozhoo geyaabi idang, “gaye niin nimashkawiz.” Nanaboozhoo gaye wiin gichi-gashki’ewizi manidoowid. Ogashkitoonaaban ji-aanzinaago’idizod niibiwa anooj gegoon. Ogii-inaakonaan weweni.

“I cannot forget it,” Nanaboozhoo went on, “I, too, am strong.” Nanaboozhoo was a powerful “manido.” He could change himself into many things. He thought of a good, clever plan.

Da-aanzinaago'idizo ji-waabishkiwaaboozoowid. Mii dash aazhawaadagaako minising. Gaawiin dash awiiya oda-waabamigoosiin sa ajina daa-waabishkizid dibishkoo mikwam. Mii sa Nanaboozhoo gaa-zhi-aanzinaago'idizod waabishkiwaaboozoowid.

He would turn himself into a white rabbit. Then he would cross the ice to the island. No one would see him because he would be as white as the ice. Then Nanaboozhoo turned himself into a white rabbit.

Apii gaa-ozhiitaad, gaa-zhi-aazhawaadagaako minising mii dash imaa gii-waabandang wiigiwaam. Akiwenzi odaanisima' megwaa gii-anokiwa' agwajiing. "Ay, nashke a'aw gechiwezhinaagozid waaboozoons!" gii-ikidowan bezhig oshkiniikwensan. "Biindiganaadaa. Giikaji iidog."

When he was ready, he crossed over to the island and there he saw the wigwam. The old man's daughters were working outside. "Oh, look at that cute little rabbit!" exclaimed one of the daughters. "Let's bring him inside. He must be cold."

"Gaawiin gidaa-gashkitoosiimin," gii-ikidowan iniw bakaan oshkiniikwensan. "Goosinaan gaawiin giwii-bagidinigosiinaan gegoon ji-biindigewidooyang biinji-wiigiwaaming." Wayiiba igo gii-ani-dibishigiishkaag. Mii niizh akiwenzi odanisima' gii-izhaawa' agwajiing miinawaa gii-biindiganigod neningibizod waaboozish. Mii dash gaa-zhi-gaanigod waabooz maanoo sa bwaa-waabamigod akiwenziyan.

"No, we can't," said the other daughter. "Our father will not let us bring anything inside the wigwam." Soon it became dark. The two daughters went out and brought in the poor, shivering rabbit. Then they hid the rabbit so that the old man could not see it.

Nanaboozhoo ogii-inendaan inaakonang. Ogii-waabandaan ishkode bapakineg gaye ogii-moozhitoon epiich giizhooteg. Ogii-nanaandawendaan ji-debibinang ishkode, ogikendaan dash booch ji-baabii'od.

Nanabozho was thinking about his plan. He saw the fire crackling and felt its warm glow. He wanted to get the fire, but knew he must wait.

Wayiiba igo gii-bizaan-ayaamigad miinawaa akina awiiya gii-nibaawag. Nanaboozhoo gii-gimoode weweni ishkodeng. Wewiib gii-bi-gwaashkwani ezhi-jiigi-jaagideg akakanzheng mii dash banzod. Gii-zaagijigizhiibatoo wiigiwaaming, epiichi banzod.

All was quiet and soon everyone was asleep. Nanaboozhoo crept carefully to the fire. Quickly he jumped near the edge of the burning coals and his fur coat caught on fire. He raced out of the wigwam, with his burning coat.

“Inaabig,” gii-zhi-biibaagi akiwenzi. “Mii a’aw Nanaboozhoo. Ogii-gimoodin ishkode.” Nanaboozhoo gii-aazhawaadagaakobatoo enigok biinish gii-dagoshing ookomisan owiigiwaaming. Wewiib gii-nawadikonewan aniibiishan baateg miinawaa gii-ani-giizhooziwag Nanaboozhoo gaye mindimooyenh.

“Look,” yelled the old man. “It’s Nanaboozhoo. He has stolen fire!” Nanaboozhoo raced across the ice to the wigwam of his grandmother. The dry leaves quickly caught on fire and began to warm Nanaboozhoo and the old lady.

Iw apii biinish dash noongom, anishinaabeg odayaanaawaa gaa-miinindwaa ishkode. Gaawiin wiikaa ozhagadendanziinaawaa wii-dibaajimaawaad Nanaboozhoon gaa-ezhi-wayezhi'aanid iniw akiwenziyan.

From that day to this, the Indians have had the gift of fire. They have never tired of telling how Nanaboozhoo tricked the old man.

Nanaboozhoo & the Birch Trees

Aabiding mewinzha, Nanaboozhoo babaamose iwedi noopiming. Ingoding ogii-zhi-waabamaa' animikii-binesiwa'. Aapiji nishkaadiziwa' iniw animikii'. Ogii-nishkaadizitaagoowaan Nanaboozhoo.

One day long ago, Nanaboozhoo was walking in the woods. All at once he saw some thunderbirds. They were angry thunderbirds. They were angry at Nanaboozhoo.

Animikii’ gii-maajiibizowa’ iwedi inagakeyaa Nanaboozhoo ayaad. Ogii-baashkizigoowaan animikii’, besho Nanaboozhoo ayaad. Miinawaa dash, miinawaa waasamoowinan baashkizaminid iniw binesiwa’ aanawi onzaam gii-gizhiikaad Nanaboozhoo. Ogii-bana’igoowaan Nanaboozhoo apane, animikii’.

The thunderbirds began to fly at Nanaboozhoo. Then they began to shoot lightning bolts at Nanaboozhoo. Again and again the lightning bolts flew, but Nanaboozhoo was too fast for them. The lightning bolts missed Nanaboozhoo every time.

Nanaboozhoo gii-bimibatoo iwedi megwaayaakong, aapiji Nanaboozhoo gii-maajiiba'iwed. Nanaboozhoo ogii-zhi-waabamaa' chiwiigwaasaatigoo'. Mii dash imaa biindig mitigong gii-zhi-gwashkwani Nanaboozhoo.

Nanaboozhoo ran quickly through the woods to get away from the thunderbirds. Soon he saw a large birch tree. There was a good place to hide in the tree. Into the tree he jumped.

Wiinge mashkawaadizi Nanaboozhoo. Gaawiin ogii-gashkitoosiinini' ji-bakite'aanid iniw mitigoon. Geget chinishkaadiziwa' iniw animikii'. Baashkwewemagad! Baashkwewemagad! Animikii' gii-biitaagoshkawaanid iniw mitigoon. Apane gii-biitaagoshkawaanid iniw mitigoon.

Nanaboozhoo had great powers. The lightning could not strike the tree. This made the thunderbirds very angry. Crash! Crash! The big birds crashed against the tree. Again and again they crashed against the tree.

Wayiiba igo bepeshaakizigaazowan iniw mitigoon. Gii-nametoowa' binesiwa' iw apii danginaminid iniw mitig-okikwadoon. Weweni sa igo Nanaboozhoo gii-gaazo imaa biindig mitigong.

Soon there were marks on the trees. The marks came from the crashing of the wings on the tree trunk. But still Nanabozho was safe inside the tree.

Mii gaa-zhi-animwewebizowa' animikii'. Geget, aapiji nishkaadiziwa' animikii'. Nanaboozhoo gii-mookii mitigong. "Miigwech! Miigwech gii-bimaaji'iyan," ikido Nanaboozhoo. "Niwii-mikwendaan aapiji gii-minodoodawiyan."

Finally the thunderbirds flew away. They were very, very angry. Nanbozho came out from the tree. "Thanks! Thanks for saving me," he exclaimed. "I will remember how good you have been."

Nanaboozhoo dash chinaanaagadawendam. “Ingikendaan,” ikido Nanaboozhoo, “Mii igo apane gidaa-mikwenimin. Niibiwa giga-aabaji’igoo wiigwaas.”

Then Nanaboozhoo thought and thought. “I know,” he said, “I must remember you every day. We will find many uses for birchbark.”

Anooj gegoo aabajichigaazo wiigwaas. Wiigiwaamikewin miinawaa jiimanensikewin miinawaa anooj gegoo ezhi-aabajichigaazo. Gaye dash nawaj gikinoonowinan izhisewan, dash waawaasamoowin bwaa-bakite'igaazowaad wiigwaasag aanawi geyaabi de-waabanjigaadeg namesing bebezhig wiigwaasing.

Today the birchbark is used in many ways. It is used for building wigwams and canoes and many other things. And for many years, lightning never struck a birch tree and the birch trees still have the marks left by the angry thunderbirds.

Nanaboozhoo & the Beavers

Gichi-mewinzha Nanaboozhoo ogii-mikwenimaan ookomisan. Ogii-mikwendaan gii-babaamaadiziwaad miziwe ningoji. Ogii-misawendaan ji-mikawaad.

Long, long ago Nanaboozhoo was thinking about his grandmother. He was thinking of how they had gone to many places together. He wanted to find her.

Mii sa dash Nanaboozhoo gii-maajaad ji-nandawaabamaad ookomisan. Gii-gabe-bimose biinish dagoshing gichigaming. Wayekwaagaaming gii-zhi-atenoon niizh neyaashiwan. Noongom izhinikaadewan Wisconsin Point miinawaa Minnesota Point.

Then Nanabozho set out to look for his grandmother. He walked and walked and soon he came to Lake Superior. At the end of the lake there were two long strips of land. They now are called Wisconsin Point and Minnesota Point.

Biitoo-ayi'iing niizh neyaashiwan ogii-waabandaan gichi-okonim. Baatayiinowag ogii-biinzowag amikoog. Gaawiin igo waasawasiinoon, Nanaboozhoo gii-waabamaad awiiyan. Nanaboozhoo gii-babaadebaabi ge pagosendang ji-mikawaad ookomisan.

Between the two long strips of land he saw a huge beaver dam. There were many beavers in it. Not far away, Nanaboozhoo saw someone. Nanaboozhoo looked and looked hoping to find his grandmother.

Geget! Mii imaa gii-ayaad megwaa mawinzod owigwaasi-makakong. “Boozhoo, boozhoo nookomis!” gii-biibaagimaad Nanaboozhoo. “Aaniish ezhi-mawinzoyan noongom?” “Onizhishin,” ogii-nakwetamigoon mindimooyenhyan, “Gigii-waabamaag ina amikoog?”

Sure enough! There she was picking berries in her birchbark basket. “Boozhoo, boozhoo, grandmother!” called Nanaboozhoo. “How is the berry picking today?” “Fine,” answered the old lady. “Did you see the beavers?”

"Ogii-gawaakwagwanjigewag aapiji." Nanaboozhoo ogii-misawendaan ji-gagiibaajiged. "Niwii-bagidinaag amikoog," gii-ikido Nanaboozhoo. "Niwii-waabamaag amikoog bimaadagewaad. Ninga-baashkibidoon okonim."

"They have chewed down many trees." Nanaboozhoo wanted to play some tricks. "I want to let the beavers out," exclaimed Nanaboozhoo. "I want to see the beavers paddle around. I will break apart the beaver dam."

Nanaboozhoo gii-geshki'ewizid manidoowid miidash gaa-zhi-bitaakoshkang i'iw okonim. Gii-zaagijisemagadoon nibiin gaye mitigoon. Mii dash wadikwanan gaa-zhi-maajii-animaaboodewan Gichigaming. Amikoog gii-gwaakwaashkwebiisewag gaye bimaadagaaziiwag. Ogii-bakitewaanowebiisewag. Gii-gichi-danakamigiziwag okoniming.

Nanaboozhoo was a powerful manidoo, so he knocked out the beaver dam. Out rushed the waters and the logs. Then the branches began to float out into Lake Superior. The beavers were splashing and paddling. They were flapping their flat tails. There was much excitement in the beaver dam.

Mii dash Nanaboozhoo, gichi-geshki'ewizid manidoo, gii-jiigeweyaazhagaamebatood niibiwa diba'ibanan zhaawanong inagakeyaa Gichigaming. Wiin miinawaa okomisan gii-gizhiibizowag dibishkoo waawaasamoowin, Nanaboozhoo de-gashki'ewizid dash wenji-gashkitoowaad.

Then Nanaboozhoo, the powerful manidoo, ran many miles far along the southern shore of Lake Superior. He and grandmother went fast as lightning, Nanaboozhoo was so powerful which is why they were able to do that.

Apiich gaa-ayekozid Nanaboozhoo gaa-zhi-pangishing mitaakamigong miinawaa ikidod, "Ganawaabamaadaanig amikoog apii bi-bamaadagewaad omaa. Ninga-zhiibaangwash, amadanishin apii amikoog dagoshinowaad. Gwiishkwishin eta igo dash wii-goshkoziyaan." Mii dash wewiib Nanaboozhoo gii-nibaad.

Nanaboozhoo was so tired he fell to the ground and said, "Let's watch the beavers when they come swimming by. I will take a nap, and you wake me when the beavers come. Just whistle and I will awaken." Then Nanaboozhoo fell fast asleep.

Nanaanzh igo, Nanaboozhoo gii-goshkozi. "Nookomis, aazha ina amikoog gii-bi-bamaadagaaziiwag?" gii-zhi-biibaagi. "Ay eya', mewinzha gii-bimi-ayaawag," ogii-nakwetaagoon. "Mindimooyewish gidayaa! Gigii-wiindamoon ji-amadiniyan apii amikoog bi-izhaawaad. Gidaa-gii-gwiishkwish," gichi-biibaagi Nanaboozhoo.

After some time had passed, Nanaboozhoo woke up. "Grandmother, have the beavers come swimming by?" he yelled. "Oh yes, they went by a long time ago," she replied. "You dirty old lady! You were supposed to wake me when the beavers were coming. You were supposed to whistle," shouted Nanaboozhoo.

Aapiji gii-nishkaadizid gaa-zhi-nawadinaad ookomisan miinawaa aanzinaago'aad wii-omakakiiwinid. Mii dash gii-odaapinaad omakakiin miinawaa apaginaad wajiwing.

In a fit of rage he grabbed his grandmother and he changed her so she became a frog. Then he took the frog and flung it into the mountainside.

Zhaawanong agaaming Gichigaming atemigadoon Gaag Wajiwan. Giishpin inaabiyan besho, giga-waabamaa omakakii wajiwing namadabid debaabandang agaaming Gichigami. Mii imaa ayaad (mindimooyenh) ganawaabamaad giishpin amikoon bi-bimaadagaaziinid.

On the south shore of Lake Superior are the Porcupine Mountains. If you look closely, you will see the frog on the mountain looking across the waters of Lake Superior. There she is looking to see if the beavers are coming by.

Nanaboozhoo & the Ducks

Ningoding dagwaagining Nanaboozhoo gii-babaamose. Ogii-minwendaan ji-babaamosed mitigwaking. Ogii-minwendaan ji-bizindawaad bineshiiya' nagamonid. Ogii-minwendaan ji-waabamaad awesiiya' ashandizonid.

One autumn day Nanaboozhoo went for a long walk. He liked to walk through the forests. He liked to listen to the birds sing. He liked to watch the animals feeding in the forest.

Wayiiba igo gii-dagoshin ziibing noongom ezhinikaadeg St. Mary's River. Zezikaa ogii-waabamaa' daswayagizinid zhiishiiba'. Gii-baatayiinowa' giigooya' wii-amo'aanid gii-wenji-baatayiinonid sa zhiishiiba'.

Soon he came to a river now called St. Mary's River. All at once he saw many, many kinds of ducks. There were many ducks because there were many fish to feed upon.

"Ay, booch ji-debinagwaa ingiw zhiishiibag! Wiinge daa-minopogoziwag" ikido Nanaboozhoo. "Booch ji-inaakonaan waa-ezhichigeyaan ji-debinagwaa." Gii-naanaanaagadawendam. Wayiiba ogii-giizhenindaan daa-ezhichiged iidog.

"Oh, I must get those ducks! They will be so good to eat!" exclaimed Nanaboozhoo. "I must think of a plan to get them." He thought and thought. Soon he had a plan.

“Ninga-ozhitoon wiigiwaam agamiing. Booch ji-mino-ezhichigaadeg wiigiwaam,” gii-inendam. “Booch ji-giizhiitaayaan sa ingiw zhiishiibag bi-izhaawaad” gii-inendam. “Ninga-biizikaan aapiji enizhishing nibashkwegani-biizikiiganan gaye nindaanziyaan gwanaajiwang mazininiminensikaadeg.”

“I will build a wigwam on the shore. It must be a good wigwam,” he thought. “I must be ready for the ducks,” he added. “I will put on my buckskin and the apron with beautiful beadwork.”

Ay, sa naa mii gii-gwanaajiwid! Mii dash gii-zaagijise. Wayiiba gii-maajii'am. Gii-nagamo gaye nagamod ge-madwe'akokwed. "Nindayaanan aanind enizhishing nagamonan. Zhaawanong onzikaawan iniw nagamonan."

My, he was a handsome man! Then he went outside. Soon he began to sing. He sang and sang and beat his drum. "I have some good songs. They are songs from the south."

“Biindigeg niwiigiwaaming ji-niimiyeg gaye nagamoyeg,” ogii-gagwe-gagaanzomaa’ zhiishiiba’. Nitaam igo zhiishiiba’ ogii-bizindamini nagamonan. Aapiji gaa-onizhishinoon nagamonan gii-maajiinid besho nawaj izhi-namadabid Nanaboozhoo. Gaawiin dash gii-biindigesiiwa’ wiigiwaaming.

Come into my wigwam to dance and sing,” he coaxed the ducks. At first the ducks listened to the songs. They were such good songs that they moved closer to Nanaboozhoo. They would not go into the wigwam.

Eshkam, eshkam, besho gii-inoodewan ani-ombiwewemagag nagamonan. Wayiiba igo zhiishiiba gii-maajii-niimiwan noondamonid nagamonan gaye madwe'akokwed. Nawaj gaye eshkam gii-niimiwa'. Eshkam, eshkam gii-inoodewa'. Gaawiin dash gii-biindigesiwa' wiigiwaaming.

Soon they crept closer and closer as the songs became more exciting. Soon the ducks began to dance to the singing and the beating of the drum. Faster and faster they danced. Closer and closer the ducks crept. However, they would not go inside the wigwam.

Eshkam gii-ani-gisinaamigad agwajiing. Gii-dibikad geyaabi dash gii-niimiwa' biinish gii-ani-waabang. Ayaanj igo gii-niimiwa'.

It was getting colder and colder outside. Night came and still they danced on and on into the wee morning hours. On and on they danced.

“Nindayaan gichi-onizhishing niimi’idiwin. Ningii-nandagikendaan i’iw niimi’idiwin apii-ayaayayaan zhaawanong,” Nanaboozhoo ogii-gagwe-gagaanzomaa’ ge agajid. “Ningii-ganawendaan i’iw aapiji enizhishing niimi’idiwin biinish ishkwaaj. Wii-doodameg o’ow niimi’idiwin, booch ji-biizikameg gegiibiingwewayaan dash giishpin inaabiyeg gegoon da-maji-ezhiwebak.”

“I have a special dance. It is a dance I learned in the south,” coaxed Nanaboozhoo slyly. “I have saved the very best dance for the last. To do this dance, you must wear a blindfold, because if you look something terrible will happen.”

Zhishiiba' gii-agoskiiwa' wii-niimitoonid i'iw gichi-enizhishing niimi'idiwin. Mii sa dash gii-biizikaminid gegiibiingwewayaanan mii dash gaye gii-ozhiitaanid ji-niiminid. "Giga-biindigemin wiigiwaaming nawaj ezhi-giizhooyaamigag," gii-ikido Nanaboozhoo. "Indayaan mino-ayaabidemigak ishkode imaa. Giga-gashkitoomin ji-ezhichigeyang maamawi-gichi-enizhishing niimi'idiwin."

The ducks were anxious to do the special dance. So they put on the blindfolds and were ready to dance. "We will go into the wigwam where it is warmer," said Nanabozho. "I have a good fire in there. We can do the best dance of all."

Mii sa dash zhiishiiba' gii-biindigenid wiigiwaaming. Gii-maajii-giiwitaashimonid ishkodeng. Gii-ayaawan gichi-akikoon, gaa-wendeg nibi gonemaa daso-diba'iganan. Gii-niimiwa' ginwenzh.

So the ducks went into the wigwam. They began to dance in a circle around the fire. There was a large pot, which had been boiling for hours. They danced and danced.

Naanigodinong ogii-noondaagoowaan zhiishiibiwed. “Wegonen iniw ombiigiziwinan?” gii-gagwedwewa’. Nanaboozhoo ogii-nakwetawaa’, “Giijikiwemag gichi-minawendaagoziwag wenji-noondaagoziwaad. Ozaagitoonaawaa i’iw niimi’idiwin.”

Every once in a while, they heard a quack. “What are those noises?” they asked. Nanaboozhoo answered, “Your brothers are quacking because they are having such a good time. They love the dancing.”

Iw ishkwaaj, bezhig zhiishiiban ogii-giichigoshkamini gegiibiingwewayaan. Ogii-naanaandawendamini ji-waabandaminid ezhiwebak. Gii-waabamaanid nishi'aad mii sa dash gaa-zhi-biibaaginid, "Aangwaam! Nanaboozhoo ginishi'igonaan!"

Finally, one of the ducks tore off the blindfold. He wanted to see what was happening. He saw the ducks being killed so he cried out, "Lookout! Nanaboozhoo is killing us!"

Ambe, Nanaboozhoo ogii-nawadinaan iniw zhiishiiban gaa-biibaaginid miinawaa ogiimoojiiginaanan akakanzhen mii dash gaa-zhi-pagadawaad iniw zhiishiiban. “Naa, maji-zhiishiibish! Gigii-inaab da-wenji-miskwaagamiingweyan apane!” Mii sa dash biinish noongom maang wenji-miskwaagamiingwed sa ji-mikwendang gii-bizindawaasig Nanaboozhoon.

With that, Nanaboozhoo grabbed the duck and picked up the flames and coals and threw them at the duck. “There you nasty duck! You will always have red eyes for looking!” And to this day the loon has red eyes to remind him that he did not listen to Nanaboozhoo.

Mii sa dash Nanaboozhoo onji-gichi-nishkaadizi. Wewiib sa ogii-gagwenawadinaan bekanizinid zhiishiiban gaawiin dash debinaasig. Epiichi gichi-nishkaadazid, ogii-pasikawaazhaan zhiishiiban opikwananing mii dash zhiishiiban gaa-zhi-saagijibizonid wiigiwaaming.

This made Nanaboozhoo very, very angry. He quickly grabbed for another duck but did not catch him. In a fit of rage, he kicked the duck in his back so the duck went flying out of the wigwam.

Zhiishiiban gaa-zhi-booniinid opikwananing gaye gii-wiisagishinid. 'Ako gibimaadiz 'zhiingibis' ga-ezhinikaanigooyan," gii-ikido Nanaboozhoo. "Gaawiin wiikaa giga-nitaabimisesii." Biinish dash noongom zhiingibis okaadimaanan atenoon biinish onooganaamaanan gaye apii baabimaadaged, ezhi-mayaagi-pizod. Omamaanjigozi apane imaa maano ji-mikwendang gii-bizindawaasig Nanaboozhoon.

The duck landed on his back and hurt himself. "From now on you will be called 'hell-diver' or 'zhingebis'," said Nanaboozhoo. "You will never fly very well!" To this day, the hell-diver's legs are up on his hips and when he swims, he paddles sideways. His awkward walk is always there to remind him that he did not listen to Nanaboozhoo.

Nanaboozhoo & the Red Willows

Nanaboozhoo ogii-kichi-wayezhimaa' niibiwa zhiishiibibana' gaye moozhag da-gichi-wiisinid. Mii sa gaa-zhi-namadabid gaye enigok gii-wiisinid.

Nanaboozhoo was very pleased with himself. He had tricked many ducks and would have many good feasts. So he sat down and ate.

Wayaabang gaa-zhi-boodawed agwajiing agamiing inagakeyaa. Gii-zegizi igo bekaniziwaad Anishinaabeg ji-biijimaamaawaad iniw zhiishiibibana', mii sa dash gaa-zhi-gashkiweginaad aniibiishing. Mii dash gaa-zhi-asaad zhiishiibibana' imaa ishkodeng.

The next day he built a fire outside on the beach. He was afraid the other Indians would smell the ducks, so he wrapped the ducks in leaves. Then he put the ducks back in the fire.

Jibwaa ani-nibaad mii gaa-enendang, "Magizhaa Anishinaabeg da-biijimaamaawaad iniw zhiishiibibana' aanawi igo ayaawa' ishkodeng. Booch ji-ganawenjigaazonid." Mii sa gii-ganoonaad omiskwaasabiin, "Booch ji-aangwaamadwaa ingiw zhiishiibibaniig."

Before he went to sleep he thought, maybe the Indians will smell the ducks even though they are in the fire they must be watched. So he said to his backside, "You must watch the ducks."

“Inga-ajidakishin. Booch ji-aangwaamiziyan ingiw Anishinaabeg ji-mikawasigwaa iniw zhiishiibibana’. Giishpin bi-dagoshinowaad Anishinaabeg amadanishin ji-debinagwaa ingiw zhiishiibibaniig. Inga-bakade apii goshkoziyaan.”

“I will lie down on my stomach. You must watch so that the Indians will not find the ducks. If the Indians come, wake me up that I can save the ducks. I will be hungry when I wake up.”

Mii sa Nanaboozhoo gaa-zhi-atood nawaj misan ishkodeng gaye gaa-zhi-nibaad ge ajidakishing. Eshkam eshkam gii-nibaa. Wayiiba igo aanind Anishinaabeg gii-bi-jiimewag owiigwaasijiimaaniwaan. Ogii-waabamaawaan Nanaboozhoon nibaanid ishkodeng inagakeyaa.

Then Nanabozho put more wood on the fire and went to sleep on his stomach. He slept and slept. Soon some Indians came paddling by in their birchbark canoes. They saw Nanaboozhoo sleeping by the fire.

Ezhi-bi-izhaawaad nawaj besho, gashki-biijimaamaawaad zhiishiibibana'. Ay, wiinge gii-minomaagoziwa'! Eshkam eshkam besho gii-bi-izhaawag gaye ogii-waabamaawaa' zhiishiibibana' gaa-gashkiweginigaazonid aniibiishing ishkodeng. Bebekaa igo ogii-mawinaawaa' gaye ogii-wiikobinaawaa' zhiishiibibana'. Ogii-miijinaawaa wiiyaas miinawaa ogii-nagadaanaawaan okaniman gashkiweginigaadeg biinji-gichi-gipagibagong.

As they came nearer they could smell the ducks. How good they smelled! They came closer and closer and saw the ducks wrapped in leaves in the fire. Quietly they reached in and pulled out the ducks. They ate the meat and left the bones wrapped in the big thick leaves.

Wayiiba Nanaboozhoo gii-goshkozi gaye ogii-nibaayaawe. "Wiinge nibakade," ogii-ikido. "Inga-amo'aag nawaj geyaabi zhiishiibibaniig."

Soon Nanaboozhoo woke up and yawned. "How hungry I am," he said. "I will eat some more of the ducks."

Gaa-zhi-mawinang akaakanzheng miinawaa weweni gaa-zhi-wiikobidood gashkibijigaadeg aniibiishan. Bebezhig ogii-biigoshkaanan gaawiin dash gegoon wiiyaasan gii-etemigasinog. Okaniman eta igo gaa-mikang gashkiweginigaadeg aniibiishing.

He reached into the bed of coals and carefully pulled out the package of leaves. Leaf by leaf he tore them open, but there was no meat. All he found were bones wrapped in the leaves.

Sa naa mii gichi-nishkaadizid! Dago gii-gawanaandam gaa-gichi-gabe-minogwaamod, gaawiin dash gegoon gii-etemigasinoon ji-miijid. Gaa-zhi-aabanaabamaad gaye gaa-gichi-giikaamaad omiskwaasabaaman, "Gigii-wiindamoon wii-amadiniyan apii bi-dagoshinowaad Anishinaabeg! Giwii-bashanzhe'in! Giga-gikinoo'amoon ji-babamitawiyan!"

How angry he was! He was starved after the long nap, and there was nothing to eat. Then he turned to his backside and shouted angrily, "I told you to wake me when the Indians came! I am going to punish you! I will teach you to mind me!"

Mii sa gii-aabanaabandang ishkodeng inagakeyaa miinawaa ogii-ashi'aan omiskwaasabaaman ishkodeng. "Giga-gikinoo'amoon! Giga-jaagizin! Giga-gikendaan o'ow bezhig gikendamowin!" gii-zhi-biibaagid.

So he turned around in the fire and put his backside into it. "I'll teach you! I'll burn you! You will learn a lesson!" he shouted.

Gii-bimibatoo enigok gichi-biibaagid noopiming miinawaa omiskwim gii-zinigwising oziisigobimizhing. Odiyan jaagizigaazonid zinigonaad aanind oziisigobimizha' gaye. Biinish noongom oziisigobiimizh miskwanzo miinawaa gidagizi maanoo ji-maamawendamang gaa-aapiji gagiibaadizid Nanaboozhoo iw apii giizhigak!

All at once his backside began to burn and hurt. He ran screaming through the woods and the blood rubbed off on the willow branches. Burned parts of his backside rubbed against the willow branches too. And to this day, the red willow is red and dark in spots to remind us how foolish Nanaboozhoo was that day!

Pakiwis, The Swirling Wind

Mewinzha igo Nanaboozhoo miinawaa owiijikiweyan Pakiwisan, gii-maajaawaad wii-namebinikewaad. Mii iw apii namebiniwag bi-izhaawaad imaa dwaa'iganing. Anishinaabeg dash, mii gaa-zhinikaanaawaad iniw gizisoon, namebinigiizis.

Long ago Nanaboozhoo and his brother, Pakiwis, went fishing for suckers. It was the time when the suckers would come up to the air holes in the ice. The Ojibwe called this the month of the suckers, or "namebinigiizis."

Nanaboozhoo miinawaa Pakiwis gii-kiigoonikewaad miinawaa enigok igo kiigoonikewaad. Gii-mino-izhiwebizi Pakiwis, niibiwa ogii-debibinaa' namebiniwa'. Nanaboozhoo dash, ge wiin, gaawiin aapiji gii-mino-izhiwebizisig wenji-bwaa-debibinaad namebiniwa'. Wayiiba igo Pakiwis ogii-mooshkinadoon omashkimod, mii dash giizhiitaad wii-kiiwed.

Nanaboozhoo and Pakiwis fished and fished. It was a lucky day for Pakiwis, for he caught many fish. Nanaboozhoo was not so lucky because he did not catch any fish. Soon Pakiwis had a whole bag of suckers and was ready to go home.

Gimooj igo, Nanaboozhoo gii-gimoodin mashkimoding, gii-odaapinaad namebiniwa'. Pakiwis ogii-biminizha'aan Nanaboozhoon aanawi bwaa-debibinaad. Pakiwis ogii-biminizha'aan miziwekamigong, nawaj gizhiigiiwitaabizod, biinish igo ezhised dibishkoo biimskowaanimak.

Then slyly Nanaboozhoo crept up to the bag and took the fish. Pakiwis chased him around but could not catch him. Around and around went Pakiwis, faster and faster he went, until finally he turned into a swirling wind.

Nanaboozhoon gii-maajaawan. Mii igo gaa-ezhi-gopiiwan, dazhi-dibishigiishkaag, dash bwaa-mikaajigaazonid. Noongom dash, megwaa namebinigiizis izhise, waabanjigaadeg biimskowaanimak gooning, mii nisidawendaagwag ge babaa-nandawaabamaanid Pakiwisan onamebiniwa'.

Nanaboozhoo was gone. He had vanished into the deep, dark woods, and was not to be found. Even today during namebinigeezis, or march, you can see a swirling wind over the snow, it is Pakiwis returning to look for his fish.

Nishiime, The Lost Boy

Mewinzha gabe-ziigwan niizh abinoojiiyag gii-odaminowag besho endaawaad wiigiwaaming. Wiinge gichiminogiizhigad agwajiing. “Gego waasa izhaakegon,” ikidowan omaamaa’iwaan.

Long ago, throughout the spring, two young children played beside their wigwam. It was a beautiful day to be outdoors. “Do not go far away from the wigwam,” said their mother.

Abinoojiiyag gii-babaamibatoowag dash wayiiba igo izhi-wanishinowaad iwedi waasa noopiming. Noomag, weshki-abinoojiiwid gii-wanishin. Zeziikizinid ogii-nandawaabamigoon aanawi bwaa-mikaagood wenishing. "Nishiime, nishiime, aaniindi ayaayan?" mii izhi-biibaaginid iniw zeziikizinid.

The children ran and ran and soon they were deep in the woods. Before long, the younger child was lost. The older child looked and looked but could not find the lost child. "Nishime, nishiime, where are you?" called the older child.

Mii igo miinawaa gii-biibaagiwan iniw, “Nishiime, nishiime, aaniindi ayaayan?” Zezikaa, biibaagiwinan ezhi-initaagwadoon dibishkoo bineshiiwewinan, dash zeziikizinid aanjichigaazonid bineshiiyan. Gashkendamide’ewan biibaaginid geyaabi, “Nishiime, nishiime, aaniindi ayaayan?”

Again and again came the frightened call, “Nishiime, nishiime, where are you?” All at once, the cries began to sound like a bird call, for the older child had turned into a bird. The sad calls went on, “Nishiime, nishiime, where are you?”

Mii dash noongom apii ani-ziigwan miinawaa noondaagoziwan iniw bineshiiwan. “Nishiime, nishiime,” geyaabi gichigashkendaagwad. Noongom idash, abinoojiiyag gaawiin odaa-inawesiiwag dibishkoo a’aw bineshii, maagizha gaye daa-aapidinenjigaazonigwen oshiime’iwaan.

Even today, in the springtime, you can hear this bird. “Nishiime, nishiime,” comes the sad call. Young children are taught never to mock the bird, or they, too, may lose a younger brother or sister.

The Boy Who Turned into a Robin

Mewinzha mii gaa-zhitwaawaad Anishinaabeg gakina gwiiwizensag chigii'goshimowaad noopiming. Mii dash gaa-zhi-mawadishigoowaad manidoon. Mii dash gaa-zhi-miikawaadiziwaad miinawaa nibwaakaawaad.

Long ago, it was the custom of the Ojibwe that all boys fast in the woods. Then they would be visited by the spirits and become very wise.

KORF

Noopiming idash, bezhig gwiiwizens gaawiin mashi gii'goshimosig. Ogitiziima' ogii-misawenimigoowaan chigii'goshimod miinawaa chizoongide'ed dash miinawaa chinibwaakaad. Ogii-misawenimigoon wii-bezhigogopiid dash chigii'goshimod. Gaawiin chi-wiisinisii midaasogonagak.

In the forest there was one boy who had not, as yet, fasted. His parents wanted him to be very brave and wise. They wanted him to go into the woods alone and fast. He would not eat for ten days.

Aabiding gigizheb bibooning, a'aw gwiiwizens gii-namadabi ji-gizhebaa-wiisinid. Omaamaayan ogii-giizizamini waabooz-naboob miinawaa Anishinaabe-manoomin. Wiinge minomaate miijim. Mii dash a'aw gwiiwizens obaabaayan gii-biindigenid, dash izhi'igood "shkenaa, odaapinan o'ow akakanzhe dash makadekeyan. Gomaapiich bi-izhiseg noongom dash chigii'goshimoyan. Noopiming gidaa-gawishim midaasogonagak. Mii dash mawadishigwaa manidoog miinawaa chizhawenimigwaa dash."

One winter morning, the boy sat down to eat a good breakfast. His mother had cooked rabbit stew and wild rice. How good the food smelled. The boy's father came in and said, "Here, take this charcoal and put it on your face. It is time for you to fast. You must go into the woods and lie on your back for ten days. Then the spirits will visit you and pity you."

Aanawi gwiiwizens gaa-izhaad agwajing babaa-odaminod miinawaa gii-wiijiiwaad iniw abinoojiiya'. Mii go apane gii-biindiged ji-wiisinid, aanawi apane dash gagwe-miizhigood akakanzhe. Mii dash, ge makademiingwed, gii-wiijii-ayaawaad iniw owiijiiwaagana'. Gaawiin gegoo miijim ogii-ayaanziin gabe-giizhig.

But the boy went outdoors and played with the other Indian children. Again and again he went inside to eat, but they always gave him the charcoal. So, with charcoal on his face, he played with his friends. He had no food that day.

Mii dash gaa-zhi-ziigwang gegaapii, aanawi chi-gisinaamagag. Ogii-baabiitoonaawaa chi-aabawaag, iw apii dash a'aw gwiiwizens daa-gopiid. Ingoding obaabaayan odaapinigod noopiming. "Inaabin, ningozis, giin nawaj zaziikiziyan apiich dash aanind gwiiwizensag. Mewinzha gidaa-gii-bi-izhaa omaa. Gidaa-menisendam. Gaawiin aapiji wenizhishing ningozis aawisiiwan," ikidowan obaabaayan. "Gidaa-bi-dazhiike apiich gashkitooyan. Omaa dash gegoo daa-gikendaman, manidoog giwii-mawadishigoog."

Spring finally came, but the weather was very cold. They waited for warmer weather, when the boy would go into the woods. One day the boy's father took him into the woods. "Look, son, you are older than many of the boys. You should have been out here long ago. You should be ashamed. You are not a good son," said his father. "You must stay here as long as you can. Then you will know something, for the spirits will visit you."

Mii dash obaabaayan gii-zhi'aanid ogozisan ji-gopaakwiinid. "Aazhigijishinin midaasogonagak miinawaa gaawiin gegoo gidaa-miijisiin gemaa minikwesiiwan. Wayiiba igo mii izhi-mawadishigwaa manidoog gaye zhawenimigwaa, mii dash wii-chinibwaakaayan." Mii dash obaabaayan gaa-zhi-nagadaagod gwiiwizens imaa mitigong.

Then the father told his son to climb into a tree. "Lie down on your back for ten days and you must not have any food or water. Soon the spirits will visit you and pity you, and then you will become very wise." With those words the father left his son in the tree.

Giizisoon dash zaagaasigod gwiiwizens ge-gizhizod. Mii igo apane gii-mawid, aanawi geyaabi aazhigijishing mitigong. Aapiji gii-zoongide'ed gwiiwizens.

The sun beat down on the Indian boy and he was so very hot. He cried and cried, but he stayed on his back in the tree. He was a brave boy.

Endaso-giizhig obaabaayan ogii-bi-waabamigoon a'aw gwiiwizens ezhi-gii'igoshimod. Mii igo endaso giizhig gii-mamadwed. Obaabaayan dash gaawiin ogii-wiidookaagoosiin. Mii igo gii-baabaabii'aad giizisoon ji-bangishimonid, ji-dakaasing mii eniwek nawaj mino-ayaad.

Every day his father came and saw how the boy was fasting. Every day the boy cried and cried, but his father would not help him. The boy waited and waited for the sun to set, so that the cool breezes would make him feel better.

Gegaapii gii-pi-dagoshinonid obaabaayan midaasogonagak. Gii-ishpaa-inaabinid dash mitigong, aanawi ogozisan gii-angwanaagozinid. Dash gii-inaabinid miziwe. Mii imaa gii-waabamaanid ogozisan niibawinid mitigong. "Gego besho bi-izhaaken," ikido a'aw gwiiwizens. "Aapiji gigii-majidoodaw". "Gigii-inikaw dazhiikeyaan omaa dash aapiji gizhizoyaan onzaam ginwenzh. Inaabandan dash nikaakiganing. Giizis zaagaateshkaan wenji-miskwaag wiinge."

Finally, his father came on the tenth day. He looked up into the tree, but his son was gone. Then he looked around. There was his son, standing by the tree. "Don't come close," said the boy. "You have been very cruel to me." You made me stay in the hot sun too long. Look at my chest. It has turned red from the hot sun."

Obaabaayan mii eta igo gii-inaabandaminid aanawi gaawiin gegoo gii-ikidosinig. Manidoog gii-bi-waabamaawaad mii dash gii-zhawenimaawaad iniw Anishinaabe-gwiiwizensan. Ogii-aanzinaago'aawaan opichiwinid miinawaa chibimaashinid miziwe misawendaminid. Mii chinibwaakaanid miinawaa gikendaminid gakina waa-ezhiwebak omaa giishpin chigimiwang, maagizhaa gaye chiniiskaadak.

The father looked and looked but said nothing to him. The spirits had come and they had shown pity for the Indian boy. They had changed him into a robin, or opichi, so he could fly anywhere he wished. He became very wise and knew all about the weather and could predict when it would rain or snow.

Noongom dash gidaa-noondawaa opichi mii madwewetood, “indinwaachige, indinwaachige. . . wii-gimiwang, wii-gimiwang!”

And now whenever you hear the robin he is singing, “indinwaachige, indinwaachige. . . wii-gimiwang, wii-gimiwang! I predict, I predict . . . it will rain, it will rain!”

Epilogue to the Second Edition:

Context and Methodology

The last twenty or more years has seen an extraordinary effort to revitalize the Ojibwe language. It is an exciting and exhilarating time with many tangible successes, especially for those of us who came of age in this environment. Too often overlooked are the extraordinary efforts of individuals a generation before who tirelessly worked with far fewer resources and opportunities at their disposal. We are fortunate in our time that our work is supported by the proliferation of state and federal funding for language revitalization as well as certain tribes, such as the Mille Lacs and Fond du Lac Bands, providing direct funding for language revitalization. The stories that are preserved in this volume did not have the scale of support that such a project would have today. The stories contained here represent a rich resource.

There were a number of speakers who were raised with Ojibwe as their first language (who learned English later in childhood) from Grand Portage remaining in the 1970's. In 2023, as this collection was going to press, the last individual who spoke the Grand Portage dialect of Ojiibwe as her first language passed away in her 90's. This volume documents the richness of the Grand Portage dialect, and we are truly indebted to the efforts of the elders and language teachers who worked hard to preserve the Ojibwe language a generation before. Of special mention is Billy Blackwell. Without his tireless work on the original books, we would not have these stories today. Miigwech akiwenzii. I want to also say miigwech to our partners at the University of Wisconsin-Milwaukee's Electa Quinney Institute for their financial support for the second edition. Miigwech to Margaret Noodin and Michael Zimmerman, Jr. for your work on the transcription of the original phonetic Ojibwe to the double vowel writing system.

I'm pleased that for the second edition, these stories are presented in the double vowel writing system (or Fiero orthography) favored by Ojibwe educators in the U.S. and the Canadian border communities that share a similar dialect with speakers at Grand Portage. Reflecting the times that they were created, the Ojibwe presented in the original editions was written phonetically, resulting in inconsistencies that can be a barrier to language learners. The written Ojibwemowin presented here is standardized, to avoid multiple variations of the same word among the different first speakers who worked on the original texts.

The Ojibwe texts offer important documentation of the dialect employed by Grand Portage speakers. It is always important to mention that dialect differences are often overstated by non-speakers. In the few instances where vocabulary differs from other Minnesota Ojibwe communities, it aligns with the Ojibwe documented in the Ojibwe People's Dictionary by speakers at Lac La Croix. One example is the use of the verb miikawaadizi in "The Boy That Turned into a Robin":

> Mii dash gaa-zhi-mawadishigoowaad manidoon.
> Mii dash gaa-zhi-miikawaadiziwaad miinawaa nibwaakaawaad.
> Then they would be visited by the spirits and become very wise.

In most places miikawaadizi means "he or she is handsome," but here the use follows other Border Lakes communities, who employ miikawaadizi to mean "he or she is clever." Again, these instances are the exception, not the norm, and as language learners we should not be intimidated or threatened by minor dialect variation, but instead use it to increase our awareness of the breadth of the Ojibwe language which allows us to better preserve and spread awareness of these important local variations. While few and far between, these minor dialect variations are an important reminder that state and national borders were artificial creations around existing Ojibwe communities. While Grand Portage shares a more contemporary history with other Ojibwe Bands in Minnesota, a longer shared history and geography exists with the Bands around the US-Canada border: Fort William, Lac La Croix, and Bois Forte, which is reflected in their use of Ojibwemowin.

While the English provided is completely faithful to the first editions, the Ojibwe is not. According to Billy Blackwell, who served as editor for the first edition of these stories, these stories were written in English and then translated into Ojibwe by first speakers at Grand Portage. There were a number of Ojibwe speakers who worked on this project, who employed a vast array of approaches. Some speakers directly translated the English texts they were presented with, while others employed skilled storytelling techniques. This is most evident in obviation, which allows us to distinguish between third persons, and is a critical part of aadizookaanag and other Ojibwe storytelling genres to avoid confusion as to who is doing what. Obviation is a linguistic term that would have been unfamiliar to most if not all of the speakers involved in the project, yet all of the Ojibwe texts employ some degree of obviation. Like any language, storytelling is a unique skill set that not all fluent speakers possess. We lightly edited the Ojibwe text so that obviation and verb conjugations are consistent throughout. Neither the original phonetic Ojibwe text of the first edition nor the edited version presented here is always a direct word for word translation of the English text.

We are fortunate to have this rich example of Grand Portage Ojibwemowin preserved for future generations to study and to enjoy.

Miskwaa anang (Erik Martin Redix)
Ojibwe Language Coordinator,

Grand Portage Band of Lake
Superior Chippewa

www.ingramcontent.com/pod-product-compliance
Lightning Source LLC
Chambersburg PA
CBHW040537170726
48295CB00012B/506

9781736551974